Kerry

Des MacHale

MERCIER PRESS

MERCIER PRESS
P.O. Box 5, 5 French Church St., Cork
16 Hume St., Dublin 2

© Des MacHale, 1992
Reprinted 1995

ISBN 1 85635 007 X

Originally published in 1976 as part of *The Book of Kerryman Jokes*

Printed in Ireland by Litho Press Ltd.

Introduction

The public demand for Kerryman Jokes is almost insatiable and certainly not diminished since the appearance of the original *Book of Kerryman Jokes* in 1976. That book went on to become Ireland's bestselling book of all time and is still being bought by many thousands of discerning literati each year.

Before 1976 Kerry was a virtually unknown part of Ireland visited only by seagulls and the odd lost tourist but the book changed all that. Kerry is now one of the world's greatest tourist centres – the Lakes of Killarney are known worldwide and the annual Rose of Tralee competition generates millions of pounds of tourist revenue. I have received many hundreds of letters from grateful Kerrymen and Kerrywomen thanking me for putting their Kingdom on the map.

So, just to show my heart is in the right place, here are some *More Kerrymen Jokes* and let me promise that I will stop writing Kerrymen jokes just as soon as Kerry stop winning All-Ireland football championships.

How many Kerrymen does it take to paint an upstairs window?

Two – one to paint the window and one to hold the ladder.

How many Kerrymen does it take to paint a downstairs window?

Thirty–two – one to paint the window; one to hold the ladder; and thirty to dig a hole for the ladder.

***

A world famous symphony orchestra once arrived in a small Kerry village, to give a concert. At the interval, the conductor complained that the acoustics in the little hall were terrible. 'I know,' said the owner of the hall, 'I've tried everything, I've even put down traps, but I can't shift them.'

***

A Kerryman was involved in an accident and was rushed to hospital. After a quick examination the surgeon decided to operate immediately. They found the cause of the trouble. A small particle of brain was lodged in the skull.

***

How do you make a Kerryman burn his face?

Ring him up while he is ironing his trousers.

***

'Which side of the river has the most traffic?' asked a Kerry councillor.

'The north side,' answered his clerk.

'Good,' said the councillor, 'that's the side we'll build the bridge on.'

***

Oil has just been discovered off the coast of Kerry. There's only one snag – it's too thick to pump ashore.

***

A railway passenger asked a Kerryman what time the next train for Dublin was leaving at.

'The next train for Dublin,' said the Kerryman, 'has just left.'

***

A Kerryman was sentenced to be hanged, but saved his life by dying in prison.

***

Announcement in a Kerry army camp:
The parade will take place on Sunday
afternoon. If the afternoon is wet the
parade will take place on Sunday
morning.

***

What constitutes a seven course meal
for a Kerryman?
A six-pack and a boiled potato.

***

A Kerryman complained that his wife
spent very little time at home.
'For every once she comes in,' he
continued, 'she goes out ten times.'

***

What do you find on the bottom of
Guinness bottles destined for Kerry?
Open other end.

***

Kerryman viewing a broken window:–
'It's worse than I thought. It's broken
on both sides.'

***

Have you heard about the Kerry referee?

He used to play extra time before the match, in case there would be fog.

***

On seeing a flat tyre on his car, a Kerryman consoled himself by saying that at least it was only flat at the bottom.

***

Two Kerrymen were out fishing. 'This is a marvellous spot for fishing,' said the first, 'how will we find it again?'

'Don't worry,' said the second, 'I've put a mark on the side of the boat'.

'You fool,' said the first, 'we might not get this boat the next time.'

***

What's the best-selling game in Kerry at Christmas?

The one-piece jigsaw.

***

Three Kerrymen were invited to a fancy dress ball.

They went as Alias, Smith and Jones.

Definition of an intellectual Kerryman: one who visits an art gallery even when it's not raining.

***

Have you heard about the Kerryman who pulled a fast one on the Post Office?

He bought 10,000 30p stamps before the postal charges went up.

***

How do you recognise a Kerry business executive?

He's the one wearing pin-striped wellingtons.

***

Two Kerryman attended a performance by the world's leading blind pianist.

'It wouldn't matter to him if he wasn't blind,' remarked one Kerryman afterwards.

'How do you make that out?' asked the other Kerryman.

'Well, I kept a close eye on him all evening and he never looks at the piano anyway.'

***

Then there was the Kerryman who thought that Sherlock Holmes was a block of flats.

***

A Kerryman was working on the rail-road, when suddenly a train came speeding down the track. The Kerryman took off down the track but was knocked down and badly injured. When he regained consciousness in hospital, the doctor asked him why he had not run up the embankment.

'Don't be a fool,' said the Kerryman, 'if I couldn't out-run it on the flat, what chance had I running uphill?'

***

How do you recognise a Kerry Hippie?
Flared wellingtons.

***

Why should you never give Kerry workers a tea break?
It takes too long to retrain them afterwards.

***

Two Kerrymen were travelling by train. All of a sudden an express train passed going the other way.

'By jove,' said one Kerryman to the other, 'that was a close shave.'

***

Why do Kerrymen make poor card players?

Every time they pick up a spade, they spit on their hands.

***

What do you find off the coast of Kerry?

Underwater lighthouses for the sub-marines.

***

How do you recognise a £5 note forged by a Kerryman?

Look for the words ILLEGAL TENDER.

***

Kerry workman to his workmate: 'Don't come down that ladder, Mick, I've just taken it away.'

A Kerryman went to a psychiatrist to get some help for his wife.

'She's got a morbid fear of having her clothes stolen, doc,' he told the psychiatrist. 'Only two days ago I went home early and found that she had hired a fellow to stay in the wardrobe and guard them.'

***

A Cork girl wanted to marry a Kerryman, but her parents refused to give their consent. The lovers decided to commit suicide by jumping off the Cliffs of Moher. Only the girl hit the water, however. The Kerryman got lost on the way down.

***

A Kerryman was being treated for years by the doctor for lumbago. Just as the treatment had taken effect, the Kerryman died of a rare tropical disease – frostbite.

'At least,' the doctor consoled his widow,' you have the consolation of knowing he died cured.'

***

A Kerryman had identical twin sons named Shane and Bryan. When asked how he could tell them apart, he replied, 'I put my finger in Shane's mouth and if he bites me I know it's Bryan.'

***

Have you heard about the Kerry-woman who tried to iron her curtains?

She fell out the window.

****

Have you heard about the Kerryman who went into a posh restaurant?

He ordered an expensive four-course meal, paid for it, and then sneaked out without eating it.

***

There were ninety-eight Kerrymen jammed into a bus, so the conductor called out 'There's no need for all this crush, there's another bus behind.' So the ninety-eight Kerrymen got out of the first bus and jammed into the bus behind.

***

A tourist travelling in Kerry ordered coffee without cream in a cafe.

'We haven't a drop of cream in the house, sir,' said the waitress, 'would it do if I served you coffee without milk?'

***

What do you call a Kerryman with eight honours in his Junior Cert?

A liar.

***

A Kerryman was selling his cow at the market.

'She'll give milk year after year without having a calf,' he told a prospective buyer, 'because she came of a cow that never had a calf.'

***

What do you call a Kerryman who is hanging from the ceiling?

Sean D'Olier.

***

What do you find at the top of a Kerry ladder?

A STOP sign.

A Kerryman bought a watch at a sale but returned a few days later and complained that the watch lost fifteen minutes in each hour.

'Of course it does,' said the jeweller, 'my sign says, ALL WATCHES 25% OFF.'

***

Two Kerrymen each had a horse, but they couldn't tell them apart. So the first cut the tail off his horse, and all went well for a while. But then the second Kerryman's horse lost its tail in an accident, so they were back where they started. Finally, they consulted a wise man in the village where they lived and he said: 'Can't you two fools see that the black horse is three inches taller than the white horse?'

***

A Kerryman arrived up at work over four hours late.

'What excuse do you have this time?' asked the boss.

'The trouble with me,' said the Kerryman, 'is that I sleep very slowly.'

***

It is not widely known that God at first intended to have His son born in Kerry. There was only one snag – He couldn't find three wise men.

***

A doctor told a Kerryman to give his wife as much sleeping powder as would cover a 10p piece. When the doctor called a week later to see his patient the Kerryman said:

'She's been sleeping for over six days!'

'Did you give her the sleeping powder exactly as I prescribed?' asked the doctor.

'Not exactly,' said the Kerryman, 'I didn't have a tenpenny piece so I used five twopenny pieces instead.'

***

A Kerryman got a job driving a one-man bus. One day there was a terrible crash and he was charged with dangerous driving. When asked by the judge what had happened he retorted:

'How should I know, I was upstairs collecting fares at the time.'

***

A Kerryman was giving a lecture on archaeology. 'Look at some of the cities of antiquity,' he exclaimed, 'some of them have perished so utterly that it is doubtful whether they ever existed.'

***

A Kerryman was reporting to the guards that his wife had gone swimming over a month previously, and hadn't returned. He was now worried that she had drowned.

'Did she have any distinguishing features?' asked the sergeant.

'She spoke with a pronounced stutter,' said the Kerryman.

***

A Kerryman's wife had just given birth to a baby, of all things.

'Guess what it is?' the Kerryman asked a friend.

'A boy,' said the friend.

'No,' said the Kerryman, 'guess again.'

'A girl,' said the friend.

'Ah,' said the Kerryman, 'who told you?'

***

How many Kerrymen does it take to hang a picture?

Thirty – one to hold the ladder, one to hold the screw, and twenty-eight to turn the wall around.

***

A rocket on its way to the moon contained a Kerryman and a monkey, each having his instructions in a sealed envelope. When the monkey opened his envelope he read: 1. Check oxygen levels in lunar module. 2. Prepare retro-rockets for minor course adjustments. 3. Examine all technical apparatus and efficiency levels. When the Kerryman opened his envelope his instructions read: Feed the monkey.

***

Two Kerrymen had been lying in wait for over three hours in order to ambush their sworn enemy. Finally one Kerryman turned to the other and said, 'he's late. I hope to God nothing has happened to the poor fellow.'

***

A Corkman and a Kerryman were boasting about the advanced technology that had been used by their respective ancestors.

'During a recent excavation of an ancient Cork castle,' said the Corkman, 'miles of cable were discovered, proving that Corkmen were using the telegraph hundreds of years ago.'

'That's nothing,' said the Kerryman, 'underneath an ancient Kerry castle they found no cable at all, proving that Kerrymen were communicating with each other by radio, when Corkmen were still using the telegraph.'

***

Two Kerrymen went to Dublin for the weekend, and in a high-spirited moment took a double-decker bus for a joy ride. They crashed into a low bridge and made smithereens of the bus. When they appeared in court, the judge asked them why they had not stolen a single decker bus, in view of all the low bridges they would meet.

'It's my friend here,' said one Kerryman, pointing to the other, 'he likes to go upstairs for a smoke.'

One Kerryman met another carrying a bag on his back.

'What's in the bag?' asked the first Kerryman.

'I won't tell you,' said the second.

'Go on, do.'

'All right then, it's ducks.'

'If I guess how many ducks you have in the bag, will you give me one of them?'

'Look,' said the second Kerryman, 'if you guess the correct number, I'll give you both of them.'

'Five,' said the first Kerryman.

'How did you guess?' said the second Kerryman.

***

What's an oscillator?

A Kerryman who eats donkeys.

***

A Kerryman went to Dublin to earn his living as a con man. He didn't fare too well, however. The first fellow to whom he tried to sell O'Connell Bridge turned out to be the owner and the Kerryman had to give him £50 to stop him reporting the incident to the guards.

A Kerryman on a building site was working at a furious rate, carrying a huge load of bricks up a ladder every thirty seconds.

'Why are you working so hard?' asked his mate.

'I've got them all fooled,' grinned the Kerryman, 'I'm carrying the same load of bricks up all the time.'

***

Two Kerrymen were in a space rocket. The first left the rocket on a space walk, and when he returned he knocked on the capsule door.

'Who's there?' asked the second Kerryman.

***

A Kerryman told a friend that he hadn't a living relative in the world except a cousin who died four years ago in America.

***

What do you call a yellow-skinned Kerryman?

The Jap of Dunloe!

A Kerryman was boasting about his brother's exploits in the army.

'He was the finest soldier of the day,' he claimed. 'Although he had only one arm, he used to rush into battle without a single weapon. His favourite method of disposing of the enemy was by banging their heads together.'

'How could he bang their heads together if he had only one arm?' asked a listener.

'In the heat of the battle,' replied the Kerryman, 'my brother forgot all about that.'

***

What do you call a Kerryman who keeps bouncing his head off the wall?
Rick O'Shea.

***

A Kerry town had just provided a beautiful ornamental lake for its town park. One councillor proposed that they buy a gondola and place it on the lake.

'I've a better idea,' said a second councillor, 'why not buy two gondolas, a male and a female, and let nature take its course?'

What do you call a Kerryman who rides his bicycle on the pavement?

A psychopath.

***

First Kerryman: 'How much did the garage charge for towing your car home from Dublin?'

Second Kerryman: '£500.'

First Kerryman: 'That was a bit steep wasn't it?'

Second Kerryman: 'I made them earn every penny of it. I kept the hand-brake on all the way.'

***

A lady hired three Kerrymen to move her furniture. When she saw two of them struggling to carry a wardrobe up-stairs, she asked where the third was.

'Oh he's in the wardrobe stopping the wire coat-hangers from rattling.'

***

A homesick Kerryman in a Birmingham dole queue, asked the man next to him if he was from Kerry.

'Look,' said the fellow, 'it's bad enough being black.'

A Kerryman joined the New York police force and was given a patrol car to drive. The climax of his career came when he gave chase to the most wanted gang of criminals in the city, in his patrol car. Unfortunately, he noticed from his mileometer that the 20,000 miles were up, so he had to pull into the garage for an oil change.

***

The Captain of a ship told the Mate, a Kerryman of course, to proceed to room 36 and arrange to have the occupant, who had died during the night, buried at sea.

An hour later the Mate reported, 'I proceeded to room 26 and had the occupant buried at sea, as requested sir.'

'My God,' said the Captain, 'I said room 36. Who was the occupant of room 26?'

'A Corkman, sir.'

'Was he dead?'

'Well, he said he wasn't. But you know these Corkmen – they're all terrible liars.'

***

Two Kerrymen bought new Volks-wagons and went for a drive. The first Kerryman's Volkswagon broke down so the second stopped to investigate.

'I've looked under the bonnet,' said the first Kerryman, 'and there seems to be no engine.'

'Don't worry,' said the second Kerry-man, 'I've got a spare in my boot.'

***

A Kerryman got a job as a lumberjack, but try as he might, he couldn't meet his quota of fifty trees a day. By chance he saw an ad. in a shop window for chain saws 'guaranteed to fell 60 trees a day'. So he bought one, but the best he could manage was forty trees a day.

So he took it back to the shop and complained that there must be some-thing wrong with it.

'Let me look at it,' said the man in the shop. So he took the chain saw and switched it on.

'What's that noise?' said the Kerry-man.

***

A Kerryman working on a building site woke up one morning three hours late for work. In his haste, he unwittingly put his trousers on back to front. Later that day he fell fifty feet from the scaffolding and lay on the ground. As the ambulance arrived the foreman asked him if he was badly injured.

'I don't rightly know,' said the Kerryman, eyeing his trousers for the first time, 'but I've certainly given myself one hell of a twist.'

***

A Kerryman wrote the following letter to the editor of a newspaper:
Dear Sir,

Last week I lost my gold pocket watch, so yesterday I put an ad. in your LOST AND FOUND columns. Last night I found the watch in the trousers of my other suit. God Bless your newspaper.

***

What does a Kerryman call his pet zebra?

Spot.

***

A Kerryman claimed he had a rope with only one end because he had cut the other end off.

***

A Kerryman on his first aeroplane flight was offered some chewing gum by the stewardess.

'What's that for?' he asked.

'It's to protect your ears during take-off,' she replied.

Some time later she asked him how he was feeling.

'What's that?' he said.

'How are you feeling now?' she shouted.

'I'm sorry,' said the Kerryman, 'I can't hear a word you're saying with all this chewing gum in my ears.'

***

Two Kerrymen were having an afternoon nap on a building site.

'These pipes make terribly hard pillows,' said one.

'Why don't you do as I've done?' said the second, 'I've stuffed mine with straw.'

***

On the first night of their honeymoon, a Kerryman confessed to his bride that he had a major deficiency – he was 100% colour-blind.

She replied, 'You sho am dat honey, you sho am dat.'

***

This fellow was given an £18 note so he tried to change it in several banks but was quickly thrown out. Finally he tried a bank owned by a Kerryman.

'Certainly I'll change it,' said the Kerryman. 'How would you like it, two nines or three sixes?'

***

A Kerryman complained to his landlady that his blanket was still too short, despite the fact that he had cut several strips off the top and sewn them onto the bottom.

***

'I'm glad I don't like cabbage,' said a Kerryman, ' because if I liked it I'd eat lots of it, and I can't stand the sight of the stuff.'

***

One Kerryman met another at the races.

'I've just pulled a fast one on the bookies,' grinned the first Kerryman, 'I'm bound to have the winner in the next race.'

'How can you be certain?' asked the second Kerryman.

'I've put £10 on every one of the horses in the race.'

***

Two Kerrymen were flying home from London in a four engine jet. Suddenly the following announcement came over the intercom:–

'Ladies and Gentlemen; one of the engines has failed and we will be an hour late in arriving.'

A few minutes later it was announced that another engine had failed and that there would be a delay of three hours. Finally it was announced that a third engine had failed and that there would be a delay of six hours in arriving.

One Kerryman turned to the other and said, 'If that fourth engine goes, we will be up here all night.'

One Kerryman was telling another of his plans to make a lot of money.

'I intend to buy a dozen swarms of bees and every morning at dawn I'm going to let them into the park opposite where I live to spend all day making honey, while I relax.'

'But the park doesn't open until nine o'clock,' protested the second Kerryman.

'I realise that,' said the first Kerryman, 'but I know where there is a hole in the fence.'

***

A Kerryman decided to commit suicide by hanging himself from a rope suspended from the ceiling. When his wife came into the room, he was standing on a chair with the rope around his waist.

'What are you doing?' asked his wife.

'I'm committing suicide,' said the Kerryman.

'Then why haven't you got the rope around your neck?'

'I tried that,' said the Kerryman, ' but it was choking me.'

***

What happened to the Kerryman who tried to blow up a bus?

He burned his lips on the exhaust pipe.

***

During the war a Kerryman joined the Air Force and was detailed to disperse 100,000 propaganda leaflets all over Germany. He returned to base over six months later, in an exhausted condition.

'Where on earth have you been?' asked his commander, 'surely it doesn't take six months to drop a few leaflets.'

'Drop them?' said the Kerryman, 'I thought you wanted me to put them under all the doors.'

***

'You have been found not guilty of robbery,' said the judge to the Kerryman.

'Does that mean I can keep the money?'

***

What's an Irish Biafran?

A Kerryman who goes to mass twice on Sunday.

A Kerryman got a job as an assistant gardener at a big country house. One day he saw a bird bath for the first time.

'What's that for?' he asked the head gardener.

'That's a bird bath,' he replied.

'I don't believe you,' said the Kerryman, 'there isn't a bird in creation who can tell the difference between Saturday night and any other night of the week.'

***

What do you get if you cross a Kerryman with an elephant?

A Kerryman who will never forget you , a dirty look from the elephant, and a Nobel prize for biology.

***

A Kerryman on a trip to London picked up two books called 'HOW TO HUG' and 'FROM SEX TO SIN'. He smuggled them in past the customs but, when he arrived home, he found that he had bought two odd volumes of an old encyclopaedia.

***

A Kerryman was sentenced to be shot by a firing squad, so he was asked if he wanted to make a last request.

'No,' he replied, 'There's nothing I want.'

'How about a cigarette?'

'No,' said the Kerryman, 'I'm trying to give them up.'

***

A Kerryman visited his psychiatrist and said, 'Look Doc, I've got two questions to ask you.'

'Right,' said the psychiatrist, 'ask me the first question'.

'Doc,' said the Kerryman, 'could I possibly be in love with an elephant?'

'Of course not,' said the psychiatrist, 'what's your other question?'

'Do you know of anybody who wants to buy a very large engagement ring?'

***

A Kerryman on his way home on a dark night fell into a drain by the roadside. He waved his fist up at the sky and shouted in disgust, 'Blast you for a moon, you'd be out on a bright night.'

'Did you get as much as you expected for your cow?' a neighbour asked a Kerryman on his way home from the market.

'I didn't get as much as I expected,' said the Kerryman, 'but then I didn't expect I would.'

***

A Kerryman who was scared to death of bombs took a bomb in his suitcase every time he flew to England. He figured that the chances of two people carrying a bomb on the same flight were virtually nil.

***

A Kerryman on a visit to Dublin, asked a guard what time it was.

'A quarter past three,' answered the guard.

'This is a crazy city,' said the Kerryman, 'I've been asking people all day and I've got a different answer every time.'

***

Did you hear about the Kerryman who took his car for a service?

He couldn't get it in the church door.

A fellow wanted to have his house renovated, but thought that all the estimates he received were too high. Finally he consulted a Kerry contractor who came to view his house.

'I'll completely redecorate your bedroom for £150,' said the Kerryman.

'Great,' said the fellow, 'all the others wanted at least £1000.'

At this the Kerryman rushed over to the window and shouted out 'Green side up, green side up.'

'How about the bathroom?' asked the fellow, 'the others wanted at least £2,500.'

'My men and I will do it for £50.17,' said the Kerryman, whereupon he rushed to the window and shouted 'Green side up, green side up.'

'Well you seem to be the man I've been looking for,' said the fellow, 'just tell me one thing, why do you go to the window and shout, 'Green side up, green side up?'

'That's just technical information to my workmen,' said the Kerrymen, 'they're laying a lawn next door.'

***

A Kerryman was lost in a big city, so he asked a passer-by where the other side of the street was.

'Why it's over there,' said the passer-by, pointing to the other side of the street.

'That's funny,' said the Kerryman, 'I was over there a few minutes ago and they told me it was over here.'

***

Have you heard about the Kerryman who set fire to his jacket?

He wanted a blazer.

***

A Kerryman's house went on fire, so he phoned the fire brigade and told them to come at once.

'Have you been doing anything to quench the blaze?' asked the fire chief.

'Yes,' said the Kerryman, 'I've been pouring water on it.'

'Well there's no point in us coming over,' said the fire chief, 'that's all we can do.'

***

A tourist staying at a Kerry hotel was awakened at 6.30 a.m. by a porter who sang out:

'A parcel for you sir, just arrived in the post.'

'Let it wait until after breakfast,' shouted the angry guest.

At about 7.15 the same guest was disturbed by the same porter who shouted out:

'That parcel sir. It wasn't for you after all.'

***

Two Kerrymen were out duck shooting. The first Kerryman took aim, fired, and shot down a duck which landed at his feet.

'You could have saved the shot,' said the second Kerryman, 'the fall would have killed it anyway.'

***

A Kerryman who became a barrister once stated in court:

'Your honour, the offence was committed at a quarter past twelve at night on the morning of the next day.'

***

A Kerrywoman heard her young son using a number of words and phrases that she considered objectionable.

'Who did you get those words from?' she asked him.

'I got them from Shakespeare, mother,' he replied.

'Well don't ever play with him again.'

***

Two Kerrymen were walking along a railway line at night.

'This is a heck of a long flight of stairs,' said the first.

'It's not the number of steps that worries me,' said the second, 'it's the low railings.'

***

A dangerous criminal had escaped, so the police issued the usual photographs: left profile, front view, and right profile. A few days later they received the following telegram from a Kerry detective:

'Have captured the fellow on the left, and the fellow in the middle, and at the rate I'm going it won't be long before I get the fellow on the right as well.'

A Kerryman went to the doctor and complained of a severe pain in his stomach.

'Have you eaten anything unusual recently?' asked the doctor.

'I had oysters for dinner yesterday,' said the Kerryman.

'Were they fresh?'

'I don't know.'

'What do you mean you don't know?' asked the doctor, 'surely you examined them before you removed the shells?'

'Nobody told me that you had to remove the shells,' said the Kerryman.

***

A Kerryman got a job as an electrician's assistant. 'Here,' said the electrician one day, 'grab one of these two wires. Do you feel anything?'

'No,' said the Kerryman.

'Well don't touch the other wire. It's got 10,000 volts in it.'

***

What day of the week do little Kerry boys play truant from school?

Saturday.

What do you call a Kerryman with his ears stuffed with cotton wool?

Anything you like – he can't hear you!

***

What do you call a Kerryman with one ear?

Half blind.

What do you call a Kerryman with no ears?

Totally blind.

(This joke is for honours students – if you want a clue, think of what happens to the Kerryman's cap).

***

A Kerryman was asked how he was getting on with a pair of rubber gloves that he had purchased.

'They are terrific,' he replied, 'if you put them on, you can wash your hands without them getting wet.'

***

Have you heard about the two Kerrymen who were caught stealing a calendar?

They each got six months.

A Kerryman was challenged to fight a duel, so he accepted under certain conditions.

'What are the conditions?' asked his opponent.

'Well,' said the Kerryman, 'can I stand nearer to you, than you are to me, since I've lost the sight of one eye entirely?'

***

A Kerry sergeant was teaching two young recruits to march, with very little success. Finally in despair he shouted at them:

'If I knew which one of you fools was out of step, I'd put him in the guard-house.'

***

A Kerryman rushed into a railway station and asked the clerk for a ticket to Jeopardy.

'Where's that?' asked the clerk.

'I don't know,' said the Kerryman, but I've just seen a newspaper headline which said "500 jobs in jeopardy".'

***

A business man hired a Kerry girl as his private secretary. One day he asked her to find the telephone number of Mr Zimmerman. About an hour later he asked her if she had found it yet.

'I'm bound to find it soon,' she told him, 'I've worked my way right through the telephone directory as far as the letter T.'

***

A doctor, having prescribed an emetic for a Kerryman, received the following letter from him:–

My dear doctor,

That emetic you gave me was worse than useless. I tried it twice but I couldn't keep it in my stomach either time.

***

Have you heard about the Kerryman who became a tap dancer?

He got washed down the sink.

***

Have you heard about the Kerryman who drove his car into a lake?

He was trying to dip the headlights.

An American tourist travelling in Kerry came across a little antique shop in which he was lucky enough to pick up, for a mere £150, the skull of Brian Boru. Included in the price was a certificate of the skull's authenticity, signed by Brian Boru himself.

Ten years later the tourist returned to Ireland and asked the little Kerryman who owned the antique shop if he had any more bargains.

'I've got the very thing for you' said the Kerryman, 'it's the genuine skull of Brian Boru.'

'You swindler,' said the American,'you sold me that ten years ago,' and producing the skull added, 'look, they're not even the same size'.

'You have it all wrong,' said the Kerryman, 'this is the skull of Brian Boru when he was a lad.'

***

A school inspector travelling in Kerry, asked a young boy in class:

'Who knocked down the walls of Jericho?'

'It wasn't me, sir,' said the boy nervously.

Furious with the low standard in the class, the inspector reported the incident to the headmaster of the school.

'I asked a young lad, who knocked down the walls of Jericho, and he told me that it wasn't him.'

'The little rascal,' said the headmaster, 'I bet it was him all the time.'

Even more furious, the inspector went to the school manager and repeated the story.

'Well,' said the school manager, 'the boy comes of an honest family, and you can take it from me, that if he says he didn't knock down the walls of Jericho, then he is telling the truth.'

Finally, in despair, the inspector reported the whole affair to the Department of Education. He received the following communication:

'Dear Sir,

With regard to your recent letter concerning the Walls of Jericho we beg to inform you that this matter does not fall within the jurisdiction of this department. We therefore suggest that you refer the problem to the Board of Works.'

***

A Kerryman and an American were sitting in the bar at Shannon Airport.

'I've come to meet my brother,' said the Kerryman, 'he's due to fly in from America in an hour's time. It's his first trip home in forty years.'

'Will you be able to recognise him?' asked the American.

'I'm sure I won't,' said the Kerryman, 'after all that time.'

'I wonder if he will recognise you?' said the American.

'Of course he will,' said the Kerryman, 'sure I haven't been away at all.'

***

A Kerryman got a pair of cuff-links for Christmas. He went out and had his wrists pierced.

***

Here is a sad little story about a Kerrywoman who tried to wash the floor.

She broke her washing machine.

***

What do you call a Kerryman going to Cork with a wheelbarrow?

A thrill-seeker.

A Kerryman who became a literary critic once claimed that Shakespeare's plays were not written by Shakespeare, but by another gentleman of the same name.

***

SOME KERRY INVENTIONS

(i)A Kerry baker once invented a new kind of yeast that made bread so light that a pound of it weighed only twelve ounces.

(ii)A Kerry doctor invented a cure for which there was no known disease.

iii)A Kerry scientist invented the world's strongest glue. The only trouble was, he couldn't get the top off the bottle.

(iv)Another Kerryman invented a new pill which was a certain cure for loss of memory. Unfortunately he could never remember what it was for.

***

KERRYMEN HIT BACK AGAIN

A man with an alligator on a lead walked into a bar.

'Do you serve Sligomen in here?' he roared.

'Yes, of course we do,' said the terrified barman.

'Good, I'll have two for the alligator.'

***

A member of the Offaly football team arrived home after a match with a leg that was black, blue, and bruised.

'Aren't you worried?' asked his wife.

'Yes, I don't even know whose leg it is.'

***

A Wicklowman applied to have his name included in 'Who's Who?'

He was turned down, but they offered instead to put his picture in 'What's This?'

***

Two Corkmen, one very thin and the other very fat, fell from the top of a high building. Which one hit the ground first?

Who cares, so long as they are both Corkmen.

***

Have you heard about the Dubliner with an inferiority complex?

He thought other people were as good as he was.

***

CROSSWORD FOR DUBLINERS

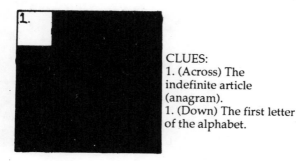

CLUES:
1. (Across) The indefinite article (anagram).
1. (Down) The first letter of the alphabet.